LORD USE YOU

YOUR ROLE IN BRINGING PEOPLE TO CHRIST

GREG LAURIE

Copyright © 2017 Greg Laurie. All rights reserved.

Published 2017

www.harvest.org
Requests for information should be addressed to:

Harvest Ministries
6115 Arlington Avenue
Riverside, CA 92504

ISBN 978-1-61754-008-0

INTRODUCTION

Lather. Rinse. Repeat.

Those are the instructions they put on the back of the shampoo bottle. Does anyone actually need instructions for using shampoo? I don't think so. There are some things that are so basic, they don't need explaining.

Here's another one. How to grow food. Farming 101. "Agriculture for Dummies," if you will. Are you ready for the detailed instructions? Here they are:

Sow. Water. Reap.

That's it. When you boil it down to the basics, that's all you have to do to grow a crop.

Now, I know there are lots of other factors to farming—weather, bugs, soil, and whatnot. I don't mean to say that the job of a farmer is easy. (All you angry farmers can put down your pitchforks.) But no matter where you are on earth, the essentials for growing food are the same: you put a seed in the ground, you water it, God causes it to grow, and when it's ready, you harvest it.

The same is true spiritually. Both Jesus and the apostle Paul used this farming analogy to describe evangelism (see John 4 and 1 Corinthians 3). If we want to grow a crop of Christians, so to speak—if we want to see people brought into God's kingdom—then this is our strategy:

Sow. Water. Reap.

In this book, I want to explain what that means. I also want to show you what it looks like in real life, so I've included a case study from the life of Steve McQueen, the acting legend and icon of "cool." (If you'd like to read his full story, you can find it in my book *Steve McQueen: The Salvation of an American Icon.*)

SOWING THE SEED

It's an amazing thing that God has chosen to primarily reach people through other people. You can't really find an instance in the New Testament of anyone coming to faith without another person being involved. Chances are, if you (the person reading this book) are a follower of Christ, you became a Christian because of the example, lifestyle, testimony, or verbal communication of another person.

There are some exceptions. Some people come to faith in Christ because God has revealed Himself to them without the intervention of another person—through a vision, for example. But by and large, in most cases, there are people involved.

Think of the Philippian jailer in Acts 16. There are a lot of ways the Lord could have reached him. But God allowed Paul and Silas to be imprisoned for their fearless preaching of the gospel. The jailer put them in an inner cell and fastened their feet in the stocks. But an earthquake came. The jailer was about to kill himself because that was better than facing the consequences for losing his prisoners. He assumed they had fled at the opportunity provided by the earthquake, but Paul and the others stayed in the prison and said to the jailer, "Do yourself no harm, for we are all here." The jailer fell down trembling before them and said, "What must I do to be saved?" (verses 28–30). God used people to reach the jailer with the Good News of salvation.

Another classic example is the story of Cornelius. He was a Gentile man who had a heart to know God. So the Lord sent an angel to him. But it wasn't the angel who gave him the gospel. Instead the angel pretty much told him, "You need to talk to a guy named Simon Peter and he is over in Joppa right now." So Cornelius sent a request for Peter to come to him, which Peter did, and Peter brought him the gospel (see Acts 10).

You might say, "Well, what about Saul of Tarsus, who was converted on the Damascus Road? God Himself spoke directly to Saul with a bright light and a voice from Heaven. Nobody presented him with the gospel." Ah, but you forget that he had his heart opened and softened through the testimony of young Stephen—the first martyr of the church, who prayed, "Lord, do not charge them with this sin" (Acts 7:60). That seed was planted in Saul's heart by Stephen in Jerusalem well before Saul encountered Christ on the road to Damascus.

Yes, God uses people to reach people. He uses humans to plant seeds in the hearts of other humans.

But you know what? Sometimes when you plant the seed of the gospel, it can be discouraging—because you don't see results right away. You talk to your friends and no one listens to you. You try to reach family members and they don't respond. And sometimes you think, "Just forget about it. If they don't want to hear what I have to say, then I won't tell anyone." Just like a farmer can be discouraged after he plants a crop and a drought keeps the seeds from sprouting.

But this is the thing with seeds: they germinate at different times. The seeds that you sow today are like little time bombs that may not detonate until tomorrow, or days later, or maybe even years afterward. Sometimes you may share the gospel with someone and they blow you off. You think, "That was a waste of time." Listen, you don't know that. Those seeds that you scattered and thought were duds may end up yielding a bumper crop in the future.

It is not until the crop is grown that the farmer realizes it was all worth it. In the same way, we tell people the Good News, and we tell them again, and nothing seems to happen—but then one day that person gets it, and they believe, and you experience the joy of a person coming to faith. Jesus said that there is joy in Heaven over one sinner that comes to repentance (see Luke 15:10), and we are told in Psalm 126, "Those who plant in tears will harvest with shouts of joy. They weep as they go to plant their seed, but they sing as they return with the harvest" (NLT).

I am reminded of a story that happened when we were in Hawaii holding a crusade. There was a father and his son that were at Waikiki Beach handing out lyers to the event. The little boy wanted to go up to some burly, beefy biker dude. The dad looked at this guy and said, "I don't know if that is a good idea." The son was insistent and walked right up to this hulking guy and gave him an invitation to the crusade. The guy took what that little boy gave him, crumpled it up into a ball, and threw it on the ground. That night at the crusade, however, the father witnessed that when the invitation was given, the irst man on the ield was that biker dude, who came after all.

You might think that a loved one, or a coworker, or even a stranger is not listening or responding. And that might be true to a certain degree—for the moment—but when you are planting seeds, you have to be patient.

Case Study

Steve McQueen—acting legend of the '60s and '70s—has been crowned by pop culture historians as "The King of Cool." Even now, half a century later, his image remains untouched: stylish, tough, manly—a rebel at ease in any situation. He's truly an American icon.

Steve had everything this world could offer: loads of money, beautiful women, fast cars and loud motorbikes, unsurpassed fame, a dazzling career . . . you name it. But the one thing he didn't have was a relationship with Jesus Christ.

Enter Stan Barrett. Stan was hired as a stuntman to double McQueen for the film *Papillon*. As a Golden Gloves champion, a holder of black belts in two styles of karate, and an Air Force veteran, Stan was one the highest paid and most sought after stuntmen at the time—and he had earned McQueen's professional respect and admiration.

Stan was also a solid, principled follower of Christ and he was able to use his respected position to begin a conversation with Steve about Steve's spiritual condition.

A mutual friend had openly declared his faith in Jesus Christ and the two men were discussing that news. McQueen became a bit defensive, telling Stan that he, too, was religious and had gone to church, but saw no need to make a big show of it. This left Stan a big opening for his follow-up question:

"But are you a Christian? There's a difference between believing and having a personal relationship with Jesus Christ. The demons believe and they tremble . . . two different things, Steve." Pressing his advantage, he added, "Just because you go into a barn doesn't mean you're a cow or a horse, any more than going to church makes you a Christian."

With that, the floodgates opened, and for a half hour, McQueen and Barrett went at it. "It was a very intense conversation," Stan recalled, "and I hit him pretty hard. I didn't let him off the hook either. Usually people don't like to be questioned like that, but Steve was open to it or tolerated it because of who I was. I could talk to Steve that way because he respected my credentials. I was quiet but bold. I didn't push my theology on anyone but, boy, I was ready when the opportunity presented itself."

Stan wound up the discussion by offering to give McQueen a couple of books that would open his eyes to what it means to truly follow the teachings of Christ—*Mere Christianity* by C. S. Lewis, and *Basic Christianity* by John Stott. He left the books with McQueen before departing the film set.

A year later, the two men saw each other again on the set of *The Towering Inferno*. Stan asked Steve if he had read the two books, and McQueen confirmed he had indeed.

"I asked him, 'Are you sure, Steve, if you were killed or died tomorrow where you would go? You're always pushing the envelope, doing more than your share of a lot of dangerous stuff with race cars and motorcycles. No one gets out of here alive. Have you ever thought about it? This is not a rehearsal. Are you confident where you'll spend eternity?'"

McQueen hemmed and hawed, and Stan told him it was simply a matter of making a knowing decision for Christ.

"Looking back," says Stan, "it was very unusual to have that kind of conversation with Steve, but I'm glad I did. I believe in my heart the only reason I went to Jamaica [where *Papillon* was filmed] was that God sent me there to witness to Steve McQueen, because nobody else was going to get to him. I know he was struggling at the time, and obviously this had been a running theme and concern in his life for many, many years."

McQueen was a hard nut to crack, for sure. Because of his bizarre upbringing, he'd developed a hard shell around himself for both protection and preservation. He was certainly a very proud man. And that pride was keeping him from admitting he needed help of any kind, including that he needed God in his life.

Stan's conversations with Steve did not produce an immediate conversion, but a seed was planted and God was not finished with Steve McQueen.

Are you willing to be a Stan Barrett—someone who is not ashamed to speak the gospel and present God's truth with both boldness and compassion?

WATERING THE SEED

Sometimes God will have you sow a seed, and other times God will have you water a seed that someone else has sown.

The seeds that lay dormant at one time of life will suddenly open and sprout under different circumstances. A medical doctor once told me, for example, that he had found in his experience with patients that those who became terminally ill were more open to the gospel. He now asks every one of them, "Can I talk with you about spiritual things?" and he told me, "I have never had one turn me down yet."

Here is the thing about the water of God's Word. God Himself says in Isaiah 55:11, "My word . . . shall not return to Me void, but it shall accomplish what I please, and it shall prosper in the thing for which I sent it." And that is why you need to use the Word of God when you share the gospel. Your analogies may return void. Your witty jokes may return void. Your arguments may return void. But God's Word never will. And as you share scriptural truths with a person, you are watering the seeds that have been planted in the past—sometimes very long ago. And still, they may not believe right there in that moment. You still may not even see a shoot or seedling break ground. But you never know what God is doing below the surface, and you never know what is going to happen.

So share your faith, and use the Word of God to water people's hearts—and even if they are not responsive in the moment, don't feel as though you've failed. We tend to think in the immediate, but you must readjust your focus to see the bigger picture.

Here's something to think about: the results you are hoping and praying for might not come about until after you are gone. The seeds that you've been patiently watering may not germinate until you are in Heaven. I have seen this happen. People try to reach friends and family members, but see no spiritual movement during their lifetime. And then when that person dies and goes to Heaven and I preach at their funeral, those people they were praying for come to faith. So don't give up. A farmer must be patient.

And here's another thing: a farmer must have skill. Some plants need more water than others, and that amount can change over time. There is such a thing as overwatering—and it can have devastating results. A prudent farmer will know exactly when and how much to water his seeds. In the same way, a Christian needs to know how to communicate the gospel—with tact, and compassion, and winsomeness.

Jesus never dealt with any two people in exactly the same way. We see Him differ His techniques when He dealt with the religious man Nicodemus. Then He changed them again when dealing with the rich young ruler. Then again with Zacchaeus. And again with the woman at the well. The point is that you want to seek to engage people. I think sometimes we will just sort of go through the lines that we have memorized and then say, "Well, I have done my part. I have witnessed." But no. The idea is to build a bridge, not to burn one. It is to communicate with a person—to get that message across.

Case Study

After purchasing a mint-condition Stearman biplane that he found in *Airplane Trader* magazine, Steve McQueen went in search of someone to teach him how to fly his new baby. His search led him to Santa Paula, a small town about an hour north of Malibu, nicknamed the "Antique Plane Capital of the World." After asking around, he was told a fellow named Sammy Mason would be the best man for the job.

Sammy was the best man for Steve, in more ways than one. In addition to being a living legend in aviation (he'd been flying for forty-plus years, having been both a stunt pilot as well as a test pilot for Lockheed), Sammy was a Christian.

He turned out to be much more than a flight instructor. The time they spent together made him a surrogate father and a role model that Steve desperately needed in his life.

Sammy was totally unflappable and comfortable in his own skin. He had a natural inner core that exuded confidence and drew the respect and admiration of everyone who knew him. Steve, too, was in awe of him. And as they became closer over the months, he started asking questions of his new mentor. What he wanted most to know was what gave Sammy the kind of serenity and peace that Steve had vainly searched for his entire life.

The answer, Sammy told him, was that he was a Christian.

Over time, they began to talk about God. Mason didn't preach or even try to persuade. He just answered Steve's questions to the best of his ability and told how faith in the Lord had impacted his own life.

"Sammy and me would fly, and he'd tell me about the Lord," McQueen later told a friend. "Flying and the Lord . . . I learned about the Bible. I'd listen and fly. It made sense. It made me feel good."

The impenetrable armor Steve had developed over a lifetime was finally beginning to crack. He'd personally seen the emptiness of the life he lived. He'd had his nose rubbed in it, in fact. He knew where the answers weren't, and now he was talking to someone who seemed to know where they were. Others had shared this gospel message before with Steve; those were seeds that had been planted in McQueen's heart. But having conquered every world he'd ever entered as an adult—from acting to driving—learning to fly was one of the last things on his bucket list. And God arranged for both the seeker and the one with the message to connect at just the right time.

There could not have been a better person to embrace Steve than Sammy, and eventually Steve ended up alongside Sammy and his wife, Wanda, in the balcony of the Ventura Missionary Church for Sunday services.

Santa Paula and Steve's new down-to-earth neighbors provided
him with the home, the no-strings-attached camaraderie, and
the emotional security for which he'd yearned so long. Now
it was up to him. Would he accept God's call? Or would he
continue his aimless search? Time would tell.

**Are you willing to be a Sammy Mason—someone who
will water seeds with friendship, kindness, and answers
about what it means to follow Christ? Someone who
lives what they believe?**

REAPING THE HARVEST

A young man came up to me after service one Sunday morning as I was
talking to people. He had some questions for me about Christianity and
we talked a little bit. He seemed open to me, like he might want to receive
the Lord. So I asked him, "Would you like to accept Jesus Christ into
your life right now?" He kind of paused for a moment, and he said, "You
mean, like right here?" I said, "Yeah. Right here. Right now. It would be my
privilege to lead you in a prayer to ask Christ into your life."

Now here is the thing. I never push people to do this. I will offer it to them.
I will say, "Listen, you have a choice. If you don't feel like you want to do
that right now, you don't have to. But if you would like to, I'd love to lead
you in a prayer." And I just sort of stepped back and prayed, "Lord, just
work in his heart." I waited for him to respond, and then he said yes. I
said, "Good. Let's pray right now." And I led him in a prayer and he prayed
with me.

Later, I checked with a friend of mine who knows him and I said, "How is
he doing?" The friend told me, "He is doing well. He is growing spiritually."
That's great.

Sometimes the role we play in someone's conversion is simply "closing the deal," to use business vernacular. There comes a point when you want to give a person the opportunity to respond.

You know, my wife, Cathe, tells me that I never officially proposed to her. I can't remember, so I will have to believe her on this. According to her, we were just having a conversation, and I casually said something like, "Well, I guess we're getting married, huh?" and that was the closest I ever came to a proposal. Wasn't that romantic of me? Here's something even more romantic: the ring I gave her was secondhand from a guy who had proposed to a girl and she turned him down. I bought it off him for 150 bucks. We were dirt poor and it was a great deal—what can I say?

Anyway, it seems to me that "popping the question" to get engaged is a lot like "popping the question" when we're sharing our faith. For some reason, people get really tense. It is like they are afraid to ask. But why should someone be afraid to ask a nonbeliever, after they have been sharing the gospel with them, "Would you like to accept Jesus Christ right now?" It's a natural question, and it's the obvious progression when presenting the Good News of salvation in Christ. Maybe people get nervous because they are afraid of failure. But think about it: what's the worst that can happen? They say, "No. I don't want to." If that happens, you say, "OK. I will be praying for you then, that you see your need for Jesus." You leave it at that. You leave it in the Lord's hands.

If you want to get married, you have to find out if the other person wants to marry you, and you do that by asking. The same is true in evangelism. If you want to lead someone to Christ, it's only reasonable that there comes a time when you ask them if they want to be led to Christ.

One of the greatest joys I know as a Christian is leading people to Jesus. There are opportunities everywhere. I was in a restaurant the other day with some pastor friends of mine. We ordered our meal. The waitress had helped us before; we were kind of bantering back and forth with her. Then she said, "I know you guys are from a church. I need to know when your service times are."

I said, "Why do you want to know? Are you going to come?" She said, "Yes. I need to get right with God."

The Lord just spoke to my heart and told me, "This is her moment." I said to her, "You are not going to come to church on Sunday to get right with God." She looked surprised. I said, "You are going to do it right here, right now."

"Here?" she said.

"Right here, right now, we are going to pray together." Somewhat reluctantly, she agreed. We prayed. I led her in a simple prayer. I didn't do it loudly. I just told her to pray a prayer after me. When we were done praying, she said, "I feel so happy now!" The good news is I know the owner of the restaurant. He goes to our church. I knew she wouldn't get in trouble.

That girl had her life changed, then and there.

Are you looking for opportunities to harvest God's crop? Jesus said,

> "You know the saying, 'Four months between planting and harvest.' But I say, wake up and look around. The fields are already ripe for harvest. The harvesters are paid good wages, and the fruit they harvest is people brought to eternal life. What joy awaits both the planter and the harvester alike! You know the saying, 'One plants and another harvests.' And it's true. I sent you to harvest where you didn't plant; others had already done the work, and now you will get to gather the harvest." (John 4:35–38 NLT)

You see, oftentimes the one who does the harvesting is not the same one who does the planting, or the same one who does the watering. We each play these different roles at different times with different people. Sometimes the part we play takes a few moments—a few words spoken, or a simple act that we perform—and other times our role is much more in depth: cultivating relationships and demonstrating the gospel with our actions and lives.

But it's not our place to say, "Oh, I'm only a planter," or "I only do the watering. I'll leave the reaping up to the evangelists." The fact is that all of us have been commissioned by Jesus Himself to "go therefore and make disciples of all the nations" (Matthew 28:19).

So don't be afraid to get out there and "pop the question." You never know where someone is at spiritually, and it's very possible that the seeds that have been sown and watered in their past are now "ripe for harvesting."

Case Study

After months of Sammy Mason's watering the seeds that were planted by Stan Barrett and others, Steve McQueen one day told his wife out of the blue, "We're going to church on Sunday." Without any further explanation, they went.

The Ventura Missionary Church had flourished under the leadership of its senior pastor, Reverend Leonard DeWitt. The McQueens sat in the balcony of the church with Sammy and Wanda Mason almost every Sunday, and over time their little group expanded as Steve brought along his son Chad whenever he visited, as well as friends from the airport and anyone else he could convince to come with him. Church became part of the weekly routine, and Steve McQueen began to change before peoples' eyes.

Sometime during those early months at church, Leonard DeWitt's preaching of the gospel penetrated Steve's heart, and he gave his life to Jesus Christ. The seeds that were watered in the cockpit of an antique Stearman biplane were harvested in the balcony of Ventura Missionary Church. Steve had become a follower of Christ and his outward life began to show evidence of his inward decision.

> Are you willing to be a Leonard DeWitt—someone
> who's not afraid to "pop the question" and verbally
> invite people into God's kingdom?

GOD GIVES THE INCREASE

There are some people who are better at growing plants than others. We say they have a "green thumb." My wife is an amazing gardener; I am not.

But as much credit as we give to people for planting and watering and tending their gardens, everyone knows that it's not people who actually cause the seed to sprout and the plant to grow. People are not the ones who make a flower to be beautiful, or a fruit to be delicious, or a vegetable to be nutritious. It is God who should get the credit for the actual growth of a plant—and the same is true spiritually.

The apostle Paul said it this way in 1 Corinthians 3:6–7: "I planted, Apollos [another preacher] watered, but God gave the increase. So then neither he who plants is anything, nor he who waters, but God who gives the increase."

God is the One who saves people. Not us. Now, I know this seems rather obvious but sometimes, frankly, we forget it. God prepares a person's heart to hear and receive the gospel. As Jesus said in John 6:65, "No one can come to me unless the Father has enabled them" (NIV).

So it is not something you or I do. It is not something we bring about. It is not through our persuasive powers or our clever arguments. We communicate verbally, but the Lord must prepare the heart of the person that we are speaking to. Sometimes we will just sow a little seed of the gospel. Other times we will water a seed that someone else has sown. And then sometimes we will have the privilege of reaping where others have sown and watered. But it is God that does the work.

DISCIPLESHIP

When we lead someone to Christ or meet a new convert, we must take the initiative to make sure that they are stabilized. Take them to church with you. Be a friend. Show them the ropes. Because a new believer not only needs to hear the truth; they need to see it lived. There is only so much that they can receive from the pulpit. They need to see it in a lifestyle.

New believers have so many questions, whether they verbalize them or not. *How does a Christian behave at work? How does a Christian treat his wife and children? How does a single Christian function? How is everything supposed to work now that I am a follower of Christ?*

Here is what Paul says to Timothy in 2 Timothy 3:10: "Now you have observed my teaching, my conduct, my aim in life, my faith" (NRSV). Listen, some things can be taught and other things need to be caught. Some things need to be learned through osmosis. In other words, you can teach certain things verbally, but others need to be observed.

The thing about making disciples is, it takes one to make one. And I think if we would be brutally honest, the reason that many of us are not taking new believers under our wing and discipling them is because we know that we are not living as we ought to. We might say, "Well, if I were to take a new convert with me, they would be stumbled by some of the things that I do and the things that I say and the people I hang out with." So your conclusion is, "Therefore I will not take a new believer under my wing." No. I have another way of looking at it. Have you ever stopped to think that maybe you should stop doing those things that would stumble that person? Maybe that new believer is the added incentive you need to remind you of the importance of living a godly life. A mature believer should be a model for applying the truths of God.

And here is another reason why this is important. There can come a point in your life as a Christian where you begin to face spiritual dryness. Has that ever happened to you? Maybe it is happening right now. Prayer becomes seemingly ineffective. Your fellowship seems shallow. And when this happens, you begin to go into deep introspection and wonder, "What is wrong with me? Maybe I need a new truth. I need a new revelation. I need a new experience. I need a new church."

Maybe what you need is an outlet for what God is doing in your life. Did you know that there can come a point in your life as a Christian where you don't necessarily need to attend more Bible studies or read more Christian books or attend more services at church? It might just be that you don't have an outlet. If you don't have an outlet for your intake, you will stagnate. It would be like a person only eating and never exercising. It is good to eat; you need nutrition. But you also need to move. The food you take in needs to be transferred to energy and into muscle. You can't just eat all the time; you'll become lazy and huge and inactive. You've got to get out there and do something with it.

So we can hear great truths and take them in but there comes a point where you need to get out there and impact others with the Good News. And in doing so, you will not only save a sinner from Hell, but you will save yourself from spiritual stagnation. The new believer needs your wisdom, knowledge, and experience. And we mature believers need their zeal, spark, and childlike simplicity in approaching God's Word.

We are not to go out and just try to lead people to the Lord and pray with them, and then say, "Hey, see you later. Have fun!" That would be like a doctor delivering a little baby and then giving him a box of diapers, putting him out on the sidewalk, and saying. "Well, here you go. It's a tough world out there. Good luck." That's ridiculous. A little baby needs to be loved and nurtured and cared for. They are so vulnerable. They are so weak—so impressionable.

And that is how it is with the new believer. They need the nurture and care of someone who is older in the faith. To make disciples is to help these younger believers grow spiritually—to become dedicated, committed, fruitful, mature disciples of Jesus.

THE MULTIPLICATION FACTOR

An amazing thing about growing plants is that when a plant matures successfully, it produces fruit. It bears more seed. And the fruit from that one plant is enough to greatly multiply and create many more of the same plant. The same goes for Christians. As people come to Christ and grow and mature in their faith, they tell others about Jesus, and those people tell others, and so on.

There was a lawyer that came to our crusade in Sacramento many years ago. This attorney was in court one day and the bailiff gave him a flyer inviting him to the crusade. The attorney thought, "I think I might go." He went home that night, and guess what? His wife had a flyer too. Someone had tucked it under her windshield wiper. They compared flyers. The same event. "Maybe we ought to go," they said. "But it might be weird, so let's sit toward the back, right by the exit, and if it gets strange we will just slip out." So they came, and they sat through the whole event, listening. And when the invitation was given for people to go forward, the lawyer did not walk—he ran to the front. He didn't even think about his wife. After the prayer was done, he turned around and there she was praying as well. They both gave their lives to the Lord. Their lives were dramatically changed by Jesus Christ.

We found out later that, after years of walking with the Lord, this attorney had personally led over 150 people to Christ. Think about that. That bailiff who gave him the flyer played a part in that man's salvation. That Christian who put the invitation under the windshield wiper played a part as well. The counselor who met them down at the front after they went forward got to play a part too. God does the work, but He allows us the privilege of participating in it. And in this case, 150 other people were affected, and no doubt many of those people went on to produce more fruit as well.

CONCLUSION

So what about you? Are you ready to get out there and do a little farming? Are you motivated to plant some seeds, water some crops, and harvest some souls for God's kingdom? Jesus said in Matthew 9:37–38, "The harvest truly is plentiful, but the laborers are few. Therefore pray the Lord of the harvest to send out laborers into His harvest."

God wants to use you! You may think, "Let the preachers do this preaching stuff. That's the job of the professionals. I'm just an ordinary person." But those who know you know that you are a believer. You can reach them. Those are the people God has called you to right now. He wants you to be part of what He is doing.

Notice that Jesus said, "Pray the Lord of the harvest to send out *laborers* into His harvest." Jesus did not say to pray that we would have more *observers* or more *spectators* or more *complainers*.

Let's pray, "Lord, let it start with me. I will be a laborer. I don't know what I can do. I don't know what I can offer. I feel a little bit like that kid in the Bible who just had the loaves and the fishes. I don't have a lot, Lord. But I give it to You."

Watch what God can do! The Lord can do a lot with a little. What did He do with that boy's lunch? He multiplied it and touched thousands (see John 6:9–14). He can take what you have and multiply it. He can give you gifts and abilities that you never had before if you just say, "Lord, it's not much, but it's Yours. I give it to You. Here I am, Lord, send me."